Mastering Habits

The Science of Change

By
Jordan Rivers

Mastering Habits

The Science of Change

Table of Contents

Introduction

Welcome to a journey that could very well transform your life. Whether you're seeking to improve your personal or professional life, the cornerstone of any meaningful change lies in the habits you cultivate. Habits are the small decisions you make and actions you perform every day. According to researchers at Duke University, habits account for about 40 percent of our behaviors on any given day. This means that almost half of the actions we take are not the result of deliberate decision-making but of automatic behavior.

To harness the power of habits is to engage in an endeavor that offers profound benefits. Not only can good habits save you time and willpower, but they can also lead to significant improvements in your health, happiness, and productivity. Conversely, breaking free from bad habits can release you from patterns of behavior that limit your potential and keep you stuck.

Think about some of the most successful people you know. Do you think they achieved greatness by sheer luck or by sporadic efforts? More often than not, their achievements are the cumulative result of daily habits performed consistently over time. These are individuals who have mastered the art of habit formation, having learned to leverage the machinery of the mind to work in their favor rather than against them.

This book is designed to be your guide and companion on the journey of mastering habits. It will explore the science behind why we form habits, delve into the psychology of change, and offer actionable strategies to both break bad habits and build good ones. Each chapter is crafted to provide you with insights and practical tools to facilitate your growth.

Our journey starts with understanding the underlying mechanisms of habit formation and why our brains are wired to create habits. We'll then explore the psychological aspects of change, addressing how motivation and mental resistance play crucial roles in either propelling us forward or holding us back. From there, you'll learn effective techniques for identifying and interrupting negative behavior patterns, making it easier to break free from habits that no longer serve you.

Once you've identified what needs to change, you will be guided through the process of building new, positive habits. By understanding the importance of routine and the dynamics of habit loops, you'll be better equipped to create habits that align with your goals. It's not just about willpower; it's about strategically setting up your environment and utilizing tools that make the path to better habits easier to travel.

Speaking of tools, one of the key chapters will introduce you to various methods for tracking your progress and utilizing technology to support your habit-building journey. From apps to journals, these tools can serve as powerful allies in your quest for self-improvement.

Moreover, we can't understate the power of your environment and social circles. The right environment can make or break your efforts. We'll look at how to design a supportive environment that fosters positive habits and examine the influence of social circles on your behavior. Understanding these external factors can significantly smooth your path toward your goals.

Finally, any significant journey doesn't end at the destination—it's about the ongoing process of maintenance. Sustainability is key, and we'll provide you with strategies to avoid relapse and celebrate progress along the way. By recognizing and celebrating your achievements, however small, you reinforce the habit loop and set yourself up for long-term success.

By the end of this book, you will have a comprehensive understanding of how habits work, why they matter, and most importantly, how to make them work for you. Changing habits isn't always easy, but with the right knowledge and tools, it is entirely within your grasp.

In essence, this book aims to empower you. It invites you to take control of your life by taking control of your habits. Imagine a life where you can achieve your goals more effortlessly, where stress is minimized, and where you find joy and satisfaction in your daily routines. This is not just a dream—it can be your reality.

So, embark on this journey with an open mind and a willing heart. The transformation you're about to undergo could very well be one of the most impactful decisions you ever make. As you turn these pages, remember that every small step counts. Small, consistent actions compound over time to bring about significant change. Let's get started.

Chapter 1:
Understanding Habits

As we dive into the fascinating realm of habits, it's crucial to grasp just how integral they are to our daily lives. Habits act as the brain's way of conserving energy by automating frequently performed behaviors, which occurs through the creation of neural pathways that become stronger with repetition. Understanding the science of habit formation not only illuminates why we do what we do but also empowers us to harness this knowledge for personal and professional growth. By recognizing the patterns that govern our actions and the psychological mechanisms behind them, we gain the ability to reshape our routines and behaviors to align with our most aspirational goals. With this foundational understanding, you'll be equipped to make meaningful changes, breaking free from detrimental cycles and embracing more productive, fulfilling ones.

The Science of Habit Formation

Understanding the science behind habit formation is crucial if you want to take control of your life and develop behaviors that enrich you both personally and professionally. Habits are the brain's way of increasing efficiency; they allow us to perform tasks without expending much mental energy. But how exactly do we form these habits, and what mechanisms are at play?

At the core of habit formation lies the habit loop, a concept that breaks down habits into three basic components: cue, routine, and reward. This loop is a neurological process that governs any repeated behavior. The cue is what triggers your brain to initiate a particular behavior, the routine is the behavior itself, and the reward is the result you get from the behavior, which reinforces the habit loop.

Let's delve deeper into each component. The cue can be almost anything: a specific time of day, an emotional state, the presence of certain people, or even an action preceding the actual behavior. Cues are essentially triggers that tell your brain it's time to go into automatic mode and which habit to use. Understanding your own cues can offer you a powerful way to take control and change habits that aren't serving you well.

Next comes the routine, which is the behavior you want to implement—or change. Whether it's exercising, snacking, or checking your phone, the routine is the action that follows the cue. Identifying the routine is often easier than finding the cue or reward because it's usually the most observable part of the habit loop.

The reward is what makes the entire habit loop stick. Rewards are the reason habits exist—they provide pleasure, relief, or another kind of benefit that will make you want to do the behavior again in the future. For some, the reward might be the endorphin rush from a workout, a sense of relaxation from a cigarette, or the social interaction from checking notifications on your phone.

Neuroscientific research has shown that habits form when there's a repetition of these habit loops over time. This process heavily involves the basal ganglia, a group of nuclei deep within the cerebral hemispheres of the brain associated with a variety of functions, including habit formation. The more often you engage in a behavior, the stronger the neural pathways supporting that behavior become. Essentially, practice makes perfect—and it makes permanent habits.

Interestingly, brain scans reveal that once a habit is formed, the activity in the prefrontal cortex (the part of the brain associated with decision-making) decreases. In a way, the brain goes on autopilot because it doesn't have to work as hard to perform the habitual behavior. This is why habits can be incredibly resistant to change, even if they are bad for us. They are skills that our brains have automated to save energy.

However, the fact that habits are so deeply ingrained doesn't mean they can't be changed. The key lies in understanding the dynamics of the habit loop. If you can identify the cue and the reward, you have the power to alter the routine. This is where the concept of "habit substitution" comes in. Instead of trying to eradicate a bad habit, focus on changing the routine while keeping the same cue and reward. For instance, if stress is a cue that leads you to smoking (routine) to achieve relaxation (reward), you might replace smoking with deep breathing exercises or a short walk.

Science further suggests that variability in the reward can strengthen a habit. This concept, often referred to as variable rewards, comes from studies on slot machines and how they create powerful habits due to the unpredictable nature of their rewards. In a similar way, introducing some variability in your rewards can make new, healthier habits more engaging and robust.

Moreover, reinforcement and consistency are critical. Engaging in a new routine every day, even if it's just a small change, can have a profound impact over time. Micro-habits, or tiny actions that take minimal effort, are particularly effective. For example, if you want to develop a habit of reading more, start by reading just one page a day. The small victory will create a positive feedback loop that motivates you to keep going. Over time, your brain will associate the cue with the new, desirable routine, solidifying it into a habit.

Let's not overlook the role of mindset, either. Believing that you can change and fostering a growth mindset plays a significant role in the process. If you see yourself as someone capable of developing new habits, you're more likely to take the actions necessary to make those changes a reality. The science of neuroplasticity supports this; our brains are malleable and capable of forming new neural connections at any age.

To sum up, understanding the science of habit formation empowers you to take control of your behaviors. By deconstructing habits into their cue, routine, and reward components, you can better manipulate and change them. Add to this the reinforcement of micro-habits and a growth mindset, and you have a robust framework for developing better habits that can transform your life.

In the next sections, we'll explore why we form habits and how the psychology of change can aid in breaking bad habits and building good ones. But for now, bask in the knowledge that the science of habit formation is a powerful ally in your journey to improve your personal and professional life.

Why We Form Habits

Understanding why humans form habits is a cornerstone of unlocking personal and professional growth. Habits are not just arbitrary patterns of behavior; they serve crucial functions in our daily lives, influencing everything from productivity to well-being. By gaining insight into why we form habits, we can take deliberate actions toward harnessing their power for positive change.

To start, habits simplify our lives. Imagine having to consciously think through every small action each day: brushing your teeth, tying your shoelaces, even adjusting your posture while sitting. Our brains develop habits to conserve cognitive resources, allowing us to perform routine tasks with minimal thought. This mental automation frees up bandwidth for more complex problem-solving and creativity.

Neuroscience teaches us that habits are a survival mechanism. The brain's reward system plays a significant role in habit formation. Whenever we engage in a behavior that brings a reward or satisfies a need, our brain releases dopamine, reinforcing that behavior. Over time, this creates a loop of trigger, behavior, and reward, making the habit increasingly automatic. This process is deeply rooted in our evolution, where predictable behaviors often meant the difference between survival and extinction.

But habits are more than just shortcuts or survival tools; they also help build our identities. James Clear mentions that every action you take is a vote for the type of person you want to become. Over time, the repetition of certain behaviors shapes our self-identity and reinforces who we believe we are. If you consistently follow through on commitments to exercise, you'll eventually start seeing yourself as a disciplined, health-conscious individual.

Moreover, habits contribute to our sense of stability and control. In an ever-changing world, our routines are anchors that provide comfort and predictability. This psychological safety net can reduce anxiety, making it easier to tackle unpredictable challenges. When your day starts in a familiar way, whether it's through morning exercise or a cup of coffee, you're setting a positive tone that helps you face new situations with more resilience.

However, not all habits are beneficial. Bad habits can be just as powerful as good ones, often resulting from similar mechanisms. Whether beneficial or detrimental, understanding the reasons behind habit formation arms us with the tools to alter them. It's about breaking down and reconstructing the loops that have become ingrained in our neural pathways.

Social factors also play a part in why we form habits. Human beings are inherently social creatures, and many of our habits are influenced by our communities and social circles. Whether it's the workplace, family, or peer groups, the behaviors modeled and rewarded by those around us can quickly become part of our own routines. Social acceptance and the desire to fit in can reinforce habits, for better or worse.

Let's not forget the role of emotions in habit formation. Emotional states can trigger habits as coping mechanisms. If a particular activity, like eating comfort food or smoking, alleviates stress, sadness, or boredom, it becomes a go-to strategy for managing emotions. This emotional reinforcement creates a powerful feedback loop that solidifies the habit.

In exploring why we form habits, it's clear that they're deeply interwoven with our need for efficiency, identity, stability, social belonging, and emotional regulation. Understanding this multi-faceted nature gives us the power to direct our habits towards more purposeful and fulfilling lives.

Ultimately, habits are a manifestation of what we repeatedly do. By decoding why we form habits, we are not just passive recipients of our patterns but active shapers of our destinies. This awareness provides a foundation for making informed, strategic changes that align with our broader goals and values.

The understanding we cultivate here sets the stage for diving into the specifics of building and breaking habits, as well as the psychology behind change. Recognizing the "why" fuels our motivation as we navigate through the intricate maze of habit transformation, propelling us toward a life marked by intentional action and meaningful progress.

Chapter 2:
The Psychology of Change

Understanding the psychology of change is crucial in mastering any new behavior. Our brains are wired to prefer the familiar, sticking to routines that provide a sense of comfort and security. However, change is possible when we grasp the underlying motivations that drive us, and recognize the mental barriers that hold us back. It's about aligning our actions with our deeper values and fostering a mindset that views change not as a daunting challenge, but as a continuous journey of growth. By cultivating self-awareness and employing strategic techniques to overcome resistance, we empower ourselves to transform and thrive in both personal and professional spheres.

The Role of Motivation

Motivation is often regarded as the spark that ignites the fire of change. It is the driving force that propels individuals toward achieving their personal and professional goals. Understanding the role of motivation is crucial for anyone looking to transform their habits and, by extension, their lives. But what exactly is motivation, and how does it function in the context of habit formation and change?

At its core, motivation is the process that initiates, guides, and sustains goal-oriented behaviors. It's the inner drive that pushes you to take action, even when the going gets tough. However, motivation isn't a one-size-fits-all entity. It can be influenced by a myriad of factors, both internal and external. Knowing what motivates you is the first step to harnessing its power effectively.

Intrinsic motivation comes from within. It's the purest form of motivation—when you do something simply because it feels good, or it aligns with your values and beliefs. For instance, if you're driven by a passion for learning, you don't need external rewards to dive into a new book or study a fascinating subject. This type of motivation is often more sustainable and fulfilling.

Extrinsic motivation, on the other hand, is driven by external factors such as rewards, recognition, or the avoidance of negative consequences. Think about the student who studies hard for the sake of achieving high grades or the employee who works diligently to earn a promotion. While extrinsic factors can be powerful motivators, they often rely on continual reinforcement to maintain their effectiveness.

Why is this distinction important when we talk about changing habits? Because understanding your own motivational drivers helps you tailor your strategies for success. If you know that praise and rewards motivate you, incorporating these elements into your habit-forming processes can be incredibly effective. Conversely, if you're intrinsically motivated, you'll benefit more from focusing on how new habits align with your personal values and long-term goals.

Motivation also fluctuates over time. It's not static; it ebbs and flows. There will be days when you feel unstoppable and others when it seems impossible to muster any enthusiasm. Understanding this natural variability can help you develop backup plans and fallback strategies to stay on track. For instance, on low-motivation days, you could rely on established routines and support systems to carry you through.

Another critical component of motivation is understanding the "why" behind your desire for change. Simon Sinek famously coined the concept of "Start with Why," emphasizing the importance of knowing the deeper reason behind your actions. Knowing why you want to form a new habit or break an old one gives you a powerful anchor that keeps you grounded, especially when challenges arise. It's your North Star, guiding you through the complexities of change.

Consider the person who wants to quit smoking. On the surface, the goal is clear: stop smoking. But the underlying "why" could range from wanting to live a healthier life, being around longer for their family, or even saving money. Each "why" has its own unique set of motivational drivers, and tapping into these can provide the emotional fuel necessary to pursue lasting change.

Now, let's discuss the role of short-term versus long-term motivation. Short-term motivation can give you the initial push needed to start a new habit. Perhaps you've decided to wake up early each day to go for a run. The excitement of making a change and the immediate benefits like increased energy levels can keep you motivated for the first few weeks. But what happens when the novelty wears off? This is where long-term motivation comes into play.

Long-term motivation is sustained by a larger vision or purpose. In the case of our early riser, this could be linked to a broader goal like training for a marathon or improving overall health markers. By connecting the daily action of running with a long-term vision, you're more likely to stay committed, even when the initial excitement fades.

Interestingly, one often overlooked aspect of motivation is the role of self-efficacy—the belief in your ability to succeed. Albert Bandura, a renowned psychologist, introduced this concept, highlighting its importance in achieving goals. When you believe you can succeed, you're more likely to take the necessary actions to make it happen. This creates a positive feedback loop: success builds confidence, which in turn fuels further motivation.

But how do you build self-efficacy? Start by setting small, achievable goals. Success in these smaller tasks builds the confidence and momentum needed to tackle larger challenges. By breaking down your overarching goals into bite-sized milestones, you create a series of wins that propel you forward, reinforcing your belief in your ability to achieve your desired change.

The environment also plays a significant role in shaping and sustaining motivation. Surrounding yourself with supportive people who share similar goals creates a motivating atmosphere. Social accountability, where others are aware of your goals and check in on your progress, can provide an additional layer of motivation. Joining groups or communities centered around your goals can offer both inspiration and practical advice.

In some instances, motivation can be strengthened by using specific tools and techniques designed to track and measure progress. Apps and habit trackers offer visible representations of your achievements, serving as a constant reminder of how far you've come. These tools can bridge the gap on days when your motivation wanes, providing tangible evidence of your journey and reinforcing your commitment.

Understanding the role of motivation in the context of habit change also means recognizing the occasional need for rest and recuperation. Overextending yourself can lead to burnout, which is counterproductive to sustained change. Building in periods of rest and self-care ensures that your motivation remains high and that you have the physical and emotional resources to continue pursuing your goals.

Let's not forget the importance of self-compassion in the journey of change. Motivation thrives in an environment of positive reinforcement and understanding. When setbacks occur—and they inevitably will—treating yourself with kindness rather than harsh criticism helps maintain your overall motivation. Acknowledging your efforts, even when results aren't as expected, keeps the fire of motivation burning.

Ultimately, motivation is a dynamic and complex force, integral to the process of change. It's the thread that weaves through every effort to break old habits and build new ones. By recognizing your unique drivers, nurturing your self-belief, leveraging your environment, and practicing self-compassion, you can harness motivation to propel you toward a life filled with better habits and greater fulfillment.

Overcoming Resistance to Change

Change, while often inevitable, can be incredibly daunting. The journey toward improved habits and a better life involves not just understanding what needs to change, but also grappling with the underlying resistance that holds us back. This resistance is an emotional, psychological, and sometimes even physical barrier, deeply rooted in our comfort zones. Overcoming it requires not just willpower, but a strategic approach to navigating our mental landscapes.

First, it's crucial to acknowledge that resistance isn't necessarily a sign of weakness. It's a natural human response. When we attempt to alter our routines, our brains perceive it as a potential threat, triggering stress responses. This is why recognizing and acknowledging the fear and discomfort associated with change is the first step in overcoming resistance. It allows us to approach the challenge with empathy toward ourselves rather than frustration or self-blame.

Motivation often sparks the initial desire for change, but it can be fleeting. Reliance on motivation alone isn't enough. We need to dig deeper and understand our "why." Reflecting on the deeper reasons behind why we want to change can create a sense of purpose that anchors us. Whether it's improving health, achieving career goals, or enhancing personal relationships, clear and deeply personal reasons provide the fuel needed to persist despite resistance.

Additionally, envisioning the benefits of change can be a powerful motivator. Create a vivid mental picture of the positive outcomes that result from successful change. Visualization techniques can help make these benefits feel more tangible and immediate, nudging us past initial reluctance.

It's also valuable to break down the change process into smaller, manageable steps. Large, intimidating goals can overwhelm us, reinforcing resistance. Instead, breaking these goals into bite-sized actions can make the journey feel more achievable. Each small step forward builds momentum and gradually dilutes the resistance, making the overall task feel less daunting.

Furthermore, employing the principle of "micro-changes" can be highly effective. Making slight adjustments to your habits rather than radical transformations can help minimize the brain's resistance. For instance, if you aim to exercise more, start with a five-minute walk instead of committing to a full workout. These small wins accumulate and reduce the psychological pushback.

The role of our environment in either exacerbating or alleviating resistance can't be understated. An environment that aligns with our goals can significantly ease the process of change. Conversely, environments filled with triggers or temptations can heighten resistance. Designing spaces that support new habits—like placing a bowl of fruit where you can see it or keeping distractions out of your workspace—can pave the way for smoother transitions.

Another powerful tool against resistance is self-compassion. We often set high standards for ourselves and feel defeated when we don't meet them. Being kind to ourselves, understanding that setbacks are part of the process, and avoiding harsh self-criticism can foster resilience. This compassionate approach not only reduces resistance but also enhances our overall mental well-being.

On a communal level, sharing our goals with supportive friends or family can provide the extra layer of accountability needed to persist despite resistance. Social support can act as a buffer, making the process less isolating and more encouraging. However, it's important to choose the right people—those who genuinely support your goals and won't undermine your efforts.

Cognitive reframing is another technique that can be highly beneficial. This involves shifting our mindset to view change not as a threat but as an opportunity. Instead of thinking about what you'll lose, focus on what you'll gain. This positive framing can reduce the internal conflict that fuels resistance. For example, instead of focusing on giving up unhealthy food, concentrate on how eating healthy will enhance your overall well-being.

Lastly, maintaining flexibility in our approach to change can reduce resistance. Rigidity in planning and execution can create unnecessary pressure. Allowing room for adjustments and recognizing that change doesn't follow a linear path can make the process feel more manageable and less opposed.

In conclusion, overcoming resistance to change is a multifaceted endeavor. It involves understanding the psychological roots of resistance, employing practical strategies to dismantle it, and fostering an environment that supports new habits. By combining these elements, we can turn the inevitability of change into an opportunity for personal and professional growth. This journey isn't just about developing new habits; it's about evolving into a more resilient, purposeful version of ourselves.

Chapter 3:
Breaking Bad Habits

Breaking bad habits is both a challenge and a triumph, a journey that requires intentional effort and self-awareness. The first step is recognizing the triggers and cues that initiate these behaviors. By understanding what sets off your unwanted habits, you can begin to create strategies that interrupt these destructive patterns. It's not just about willpower; it's about designing an environment and mindset that give you the best chance to succeed. Reflect on your routines, identify the moments when you're most vulnerable, and explore alternative actions that align with the person you aspire to be. Remember, breaking a bad habit isn't a one-time event; it's a continuous process that involves making mindful choices every day. Empower yourself with the tools and insight you need, and embrace the small victories along the way as they add up to meaningful change.

Identifying Triggers and Cues

One of the most fundamental steps in breaking bad habits is identifying the triggers and cues that set them in motion. Without understanding what initiates these unwanted behaviors, it becomes nearly impossible to combat them effectively. Imagine trying to rid yourself of a fever without knowing what caused the infection in the first place. The same principle applies to habits: you must first identify the root causes to address the symptoms successfully.

Our daily lives are filled with a multitude of stimuli, many of which we encounter without conscious awareness. These stimuli act as triggers or cues for our habits. A trigger is any event or situation that sets off a series of behaviors, much like a traffic light turning green signals drivers to move forward. Cues are the specific elements in our environment or within ourselves that signal the brain to initiate a particular habit. They can be sights, sounds, emotional states, or even the time of day.

For instance, if you find yourself reaching for junk food every time you're stressed, stress may be your trigger, and the sight of your pantry serves as a cue. Conversely, if your bad habit is procrastination, your trigger might be a daunting task that you don't want to start, and the cue could be the specific time of day when you typically feel the most overwhelmed. By identifying these elements, you can begin to understand the underlying mechanics of your behaviors.

Let's delve into a practical approach to identifying your own triggers and cues. Begin by keeping a habit journal. Over the course of a week or two, make a note every time you engage in the habit you want to break. Record what you were doing immediately before, what time it was, who you were with, and what emotional state you were in. This meticulous recording will help you identify patterns and commonalities that highlight your triggers and cues.

Take Jane, for example, a professional who found herself habitually checking her phone multiple times an hour. By recording her actions, she noticed that her phone-checking habit spiked every time she felt anxiety about a looming deadline. The anxiety was her trigger, and the cue was her workspace that made her feel overwhelmed. Once Jane recognized this, she could create a strategy to manage her anxiety and reframe her workspace, thereby reducing her phone-checking habit.

Identifying triggers and cues also involves looking at your sensory experiences. Are there particular sights, sounds, or smells that precede your bad habits? It's fascinating how our brains can associate specific sensory inputs with certain behaviors. For example, the smell of popcorn might trigger a snacking habit because your brain associates it with watching movies and, subsequently, eating mindlessly. Understanding these associations can give you the leverage to change them.

Another critical area to examine is your emotional states. Emotional triggers play a significant role in the perpetuation of bad habits. Feelings of stress, boredom, anger, or sadness can all serve as catalysts for behaviors you want to eliminate. Recognizing these emotional states can be challenging, but it's necessary for breaking the cycle. Ask yourself, "What am I feeling right now?" each time you notice the urge to engage in the habit. Over time, you'll become more adept at pinpointing which emotions are driving your actions.

It's also worth exploring social triggers. Sometimes the people you are around can act as cues for your habits. For example, maybe you smoke when you're with a particular group of friends, or you find yourself gossiping every time you meet a specific colleague. Social dynamics are powerful influences on behavior, and recognizing these influences helps you develop strategies to mitigate them.

Don't underestimate the importance of the environment itself. Physical spaces can contain countless cues that trigger your bad habits. A messy desk might prompt procrastination, while a cozy living room could lead to excessive TV watching. By altering your environment, you can eliminate some of these physical cues or replace them with triggers for more positive behaviors.

Moreover, the time of day can be a significant cue. Many habits are bound tightly to our daily routines. You might find that you're more likely to indulge in unhealthy snacks in the late afternoon when your energy levels dip, or that you're more prone to skip workouts early in the morning when getting out of bed feels like a Herculean task. By identifying these time-bound cues, you can plan interventions to disrupt the habit loop.

After identifying your triggers and cues, it's crucial to create a plan for how to deal with them. This plan involves both avoiding known triggers and introducing new, positive cues that encourage better habits. For example, if you find that stress triggers your unhealthy snacking, consider implementing a new routine of deep breathing exercises or a short walk whenever you start feeling stressed. These new actions can serve as positive cues that redirect your behavior in a more constructive direction.

Understanding your triggers and cues opens up a plethora of opportunities to replace bad habits with good ones. This knowledge serves as a foundation upon which you can build new, healthier habits that contribute to your overall well-being. By recognizing and managing the elements that influence your behavior, you empower yourself to take control and make lasting changes. Remember, it's about creating an environment—both internal and external—that supports the life you want to live.

This journey of identifying and managing your triggers and cues will be ongoing. It requires persistence and self-reflection. Yet, the effort is worthwhile because understanding the roots of your habits enables you to disrupt patterns that no longer serve you and replace them with ones that align with your goals. Your capacity for change is immense, and by gaining insights into what drives your behavior, you're already taking a significant step towards a better life.

Strategies for Interrupting Patterns

Breaking bad habits often hinges on our ability to disrupt the cycles that keep them alive. The brain loves efficiency, and habits are its way of automating frequently performed actions. To combat this inertia, it's essential to implement strategies that can effectively interrupt these patterns. Understanding and utilizing these tactics can turn the tide in favor of better behavior patterns that align with your personal and professional aspirations.

First, let's discuss the concept of "pattern interruption." This strategy involves breaking the chain of events that lead to a bad habit. When we perform an action out of habit, it often follows a predictable sequence: a trigger, the routine, and the reward. To disrupt this flow, we have to interfere with one or more of these elements. For instance, if you habitually reach for a sugary snack every afternoon, identifying and altering the trigger — perhaps boredom or an afternoon energy slump — can stop the habit in its tracks.

One effective method is to introduce a "pause" in your routine. When you recognize a trigger, take a moment to pause and reflect on what you're about to do. This brief moment of mindfulness can make a significant difference. By simply stopping and asking yourself, "Do I really want to do this?" or "Is there a better way to handle this situation?" you create a window of opportunity to choose a different action.

An alternative technique is substitution. Instead of merely trying to discontinue a bad habit, replace it with a healthier one that satisfies the same need. For example, if you tend to smoke a cigarette to relieve stress, try substituting that behavior with a quick workout, five minutes of deep breathing, or even a conversation with a supportive friend. The key is to find a replacement that offers a similar reward but in a beneficial way.

Another powerful strategy is changing your environment. Our surroundings have a significant impact on our behavior. If you always eat junk food while watching TV, perhaps you can rearrange your living room or remove the unhealthy snacks from the immediate vicinity. The goal is to create friction for the bad habit and lower the barrier for the desired behavior. The harder it is to engage in the old habit, the less likely you are to fall back into it.

Redefining your "why" can also be remarkably transformative. Remind yourself regularly about why you want to break the habit in the first place. Are you aiming for better health, more productivity, or improved relationships? Keep your motivations visible and compelling. Write them down and place them where you'll see them frequently. This constant reinforcement can keep you aligned with your long-term goals.

Public accountability can serve as another compelling approach. Share your goals with someone you trust or even engage in social circles that encourage positive change. Online communities, support groups, or even simple buddy systems can offer accountability and support. When others are aware of your objectives, you'll likely feel a greater sense of responsibility to maintain your commitments.

Let's not underestimate the power of gradual change. Trying to overhaul multiple habits at once can be overwhelming and counterproductive. Focus on one habit at a time. Smaller, incremental changes are often more sustainable long-term. Celebrate small victories along the way to keep your motivation high and reinforce your progress.

Lastly, developing an awareness of your internal dialogue can be pivotal. Self-talk can either sabotage your efforts or empower you to keep going. Replace negative, defeatist thoughts with positive affirmations. Instead of telling yourself, "I'll never be able to break this habit," reframe it to "I am capable of changing my behaviors and I am getting better every day."

In summary, breaking bad habits requires a multifaceted approach. By interrupting established patterns through pausing, substituting, environmental changes, redefining your "why," leveraging public accountability, making gradual change, and cultivating positive self-talk, you equip yourself with a robust set of tools for meaningful transformation. The journey isn't always easy, but with these strategies, mov-moving towards a better, more fulfilling life becomes achievable.

Chapter 4:
Building Good Habits

Embarking on the journey to build good habits is akin to setting the foundation for a prosperous and fulfilling life. It's crucial to acknowledge that routines are the backbone of these habits, offering a framework within which they can flourish. By intentionally creating new habit loops, we can systematically integrate positive behaviors into our daily lives. This process isn't just about repetition; it's about consistency and commitment. Each small, deliberate action composes the larger picture of personal growth and professional excellence. By understanding the importance of routine and designing loops that align with our goals, we empower ourselves to take control of our habits. This conscious effort to cultivate good habits ultimately leads to a life of improved well-being, productivity, and satisfaction.

The Importance of Routine

When it comes to building good habits, routine is your best ally. It's the glue that holds your habits together, making it easier to follow through on the actions you want to embed into your daily life. Without routine, even the best-laid plans can fall apart. So what makes routine so essential?

First, routines provide structure. They give your day a framework, making it easier to slot in those new habits you're trying to cultivate. Think of your day like a house; your routines are the walls and floors that provide space for your new habits to live in. By creating a consistent structure, routines free your mind from having to constantly decide what to do next. This frees up mental energy, which you can then use to focus on more complex tasks.

Beyond structure, routines offer a sense of stability. In a world that's constantly changing, a reliable routine can be a comforting constant. This stability is crucial because it provides a solid foundation upon which to build new habits. When everything else feels uncertain, a routine can remind you that there's at least one aspect of your life you can control. Knowing that your morning starts with meditation or a workout can give you the reassurance needed to tackle the day's unpredictability.

This is important because human beings are creatures of habit. We thrive on predictability and find comfort in the familiar. By setting up routines, you're essentially tapping into a natural tendency, making it easier to adopt new habits. For example, if you want to incorporate exercise into your day, it's more feasible if you associate it with a certain time or trigger—like a morning run immediately after waking up.

Furthermore, routine helps in measuring progress. It's tough to measure how much you've improved if your practices are scattered and disorganized. Consistent routines allow you to track your actions, reflect on your performance, and adjust accordingly. If you read every night before bed, you can clearly see how many books you've completed within a month, giving you a tangible sense of accomplishment.

In addition to providing structure and stability, routines minimize stress and decision fatigue. Every decision we make throughout the day drains a bit of our mental energy. By having a set routine, you eliminate the need to make decisions about the basics. You've probably heard of successful individuals like CEOs wearing the same outfit every day. It's not about fashion but rather about reducing decision fatigue, allowing them to focus their decision-making power on more critical choices.

Another huge advantage of routine is that it promotes self-discipline. When you follow a regular schedule, you're training yourself to be disciplined. You're conditioning your mind and body to act in a certain way at a certain time. This increased discipline will spill over into other aspects of your life, making it easier to stick to other habits or tackle challenges that require persistence.

It's also worth noting that routines build momentum. The more you stick to a routine, the easier it becomes to sustain it. It's like pushing a snowball down a hill; the initial effort is substantial, but once you get it going, it starts to roll on its own. This kind of momentum is invaluable when you're trying to build long-lasting habits. The longer you stick to a routine, the less effort it takes to maintain it.

But what happens when you break a routine? Life is unpredictable, and disruptions are inevitable. The key is to plan for these moments. Have a 'restart' mechanism that allows you to get back on track. It's not the break in the routine that destroys a habit but the failure to get back into it. Therefore, plan for contingencies. If you miss your morning workout, can you squeeze in a shorter session later in the day? Contingency planning ensures that one slip won't turn into a fall.

Personalizing your routine is another critical factor. What works for someone else might not work for you. It's important to tailor routines to fit your lifestyle, preferences, and needs. Some people thrive on an early morning routine while others may find they're more productive in the evening. The key is to experiment, find what works best for you, and stick to it. Customization makes it more likely that you'll adhere to the routine in the long run.

Routines don't have to be dull or monotonous. They can bring a sense of enrichment to your life by ensuring you're consistently doing activities that contribute to your well-being. If you enjoy reading, integrating it into your nightly routine means you get to do something you love every day, making your life more enjoyable and fulfilling.

On a broader scale, routines can even contribute to your identity. They help define who you are and what you stand for. If you have a routine that includes exercise, healthy eating, and reading every day, over time, you'll start to see yourself as a fit, healthy, and well-read person. This positive self-identity can act as a strong motivating factor to stick to your habits and routines.

The psychological benefits can't be overstated either. Routines offer a sense of purpose and control. Starting your day with a clear plan can make you feel accomplished before you've even left the house. This sense of early achievement can set a positive tone for the rest of the day, boosting both your mood and productivity.

As you can see, the importance of routine lies in its ability to provide structure, stability, and momentum. It's an essential building block for creating and maintaining good habits. Whether you're aiming to improve your physical health, mental well-being, or professional skills, a well-established routine can make the journey not just manageable, but also enjoyable.

Ultimately, routines are your roadmap to achieving your goals. They break down your big, ambitious dreams into daily, achievable actions. By sticking to a routine, you're not just building good habits; you're crafting a lifestyle that aligns with your values and aspirations. Take control of your routines, and you'll find it's much easier to take control of your life.

Creating New Habit Loops

Forming new habits isn't just about willpower or motivation; it's an intricate dance of cues, routines, and rewards. When we understand this dynamic, we can better manipulate these elements to engrain positive behaviors deeply into our daily life. But before diving into the mechanics, let's first appreciate why this concept is fundamentally transformative.

Imagine a habit loop as a three-part process. First, a cue triggers the behavior. This could be as simple as walking into the kitchen, which cues the habit loop of making a cup of coffee. Second, the routine is the behavior itself—in our coffee example, this is the act of brewing and drinking the coffee. Lastly, the reward is the satisfaction you derive from the behavior, like the energizing feeling from caffeine. By breaking this process down, we can start to see where interventions can be made to foster new, beneficial habits.

Creating new habit loops involves identifying a cue, designing a routine, and defining a reward. A reliable cue should be specific and consistent. For instance, setting an alarm at 7 a.m. each day can serve as a cue to begin a morning exercise routine. Consistency is key here; the more regularly you encounter the cue, the more likely the habit will stick.

The routine—the second part of the loop—needs careful crafting. It should be straightforward and uncomplicated initially, to avoid overwhelming your willpower. If your goal is to exercise in the morning, start with a 5-minute routine. As the habit solidifies, gradually increase the time or intensity. Complexity can be counterproductive in the beginning stages.

Reward plays a pivotal role and must be compelling enough to keep you coming back to the routine. The brain thrives on rewards— they reinforce the behavior and make you more likely to repeat it. For our exercise example, immediate rewards could be a delicious post-workout smoothie or a few minutes of relaxing with a good book. Long-term rewards, like noticing improvements in your health and stamina, will help sustain the habit over time.

It's also crucial to note that creating new habit loops involves some experimentation. You may need to tweak your cues, routines, and rewards to find what works best for you. Don't be discouraged if your first attempt isn't perfect; refine and adjust as needed. Tracking your progress can provide valuable insights into what's effective and what needs adjustment.

Moreover, embedding these new habit loops within your existing routines can boost their success. Known as 'stacking habits,' this technique leverages the momentum of established behaviors. For example, if you already have a strong habit of brushing your teeth every morning, you could "stack" a new habit of doing ten pushups right afterward. The existing habit provides a stable anchor for the new behavior.

Simplifying the initiation of positive behaviors also aids in creating new habit loops. Set your workout clothes out the night before if your goal is to exercise in the morning. By removing barriers, you're making it easier to follow through with the desired routine. This concept, often termed as 'reducing friction,' can be applied to various habits you want to adopt.

Incorporating social elements into your habit loops can further amplify their power. Human beings are inherently social creatures, and we often thrive in community environments. Whether it's a workout group, a book club, or an accountability partner, engaging with others on your journey can provide mutual motivation and support. The sense of belonging and the positive peer pressure can greatly enhance your commitment to the new habit loop.

External rewards like social recognition and internal rewards like personal satisfaction work synergistically. Recognizing and celebrating small wins can foster a positive feedback loop. Each time you acknowledge your progress, you reinforce the habit's integration into your lifestyle. Make it a point to reward yourself, even if it's just mentally acknowledging your achievement.

As you deepen these new habits, they can become more automatic, freeing up cognitive resources for other tasks and decisions. This shift from conscious effort to automaticity is what makes habits so power-ful in transforming our lives. Once established, these positive habit loops require minimal effort to maintain.

It's also beneficial to visualize the long-term impact of your new habits. Ask yourself how these changes will affect your personal and professional life in the years to come. This vision can provide strong motivational fuel as you work through the more challenging initial phases of habit formation.

Failure is an inevitable part of the journey, and understanding this can help you remain resilient. Don't view setbacks as failures but as learning opportunities. Reflect on what went wrong and how you might handle similar situations differently in the future. Adjust your habit loop accordingly and keep moving forward.

Lastly, remember that the ultimate goal of creating new habit loops is to enhance the quality of your life. It's not about perfection but progress. Each small, positive change compounds over time, lead-ing to significant improvements in both your personal and profess-ional realms. By mastering the art of habit loops, you're setting the foundation for a more productive, fulfilling, and enriching life.

Chapter 5:
Tools and Techniques

As we delve into the practicalities of transforming your life through habits, "Tools and Techniques" serves as your toolkit to success. It's about equipping yourself with the right instruments that make habit formation and maintenance as seamless as possible. Think of this chapter as your go-to resource for actionable strategies. Whether it's habit tracking, which allows you to visually measure your progress and stay motivated, or leveraging the latest technology to streamline and support your journey, these methods will simplify the path to better habits. The right tools and techniques can act as catalysts, making the seemingly daunting process of behavioral change much more manageable and even enjoyable. So, let's move forward and explore the best ways to set yourself up for lasting success.

Habit Tracking

Imagine setting a goal to read more books, exercise regularly, or even drink more water, yet you find yourself falling short time and time again. This is where habit tracking can become a game changer. When you track your habits, you create a system of accountability and visibility that helps you stay on course. But don't just think of habit tracking as another chore on your to-do list. It's an insightful and empowering tool that brings you closer to understanding your own behaviors.

Habit tracking involves the process of recording your progress in achieving a specific behavior or set of behaviors. It provides tangible evidence of your efforts, allowing you to see how well you're sticking to your new habits and where you might need to adjust. The act of tracking itself often serves as an additional motivator, nudging you to stay consistent. Consistency, after all, is the bedrock of habit formation.

The first step in effective habit tracking is to decide what you want to track. It's important to be specific. Instead of setting a vague goal like "exercise more," consider setting a concrete goal such as "go for a 30-minute jog three days a week." This specificity allows for clearer tracking and a more defined sense of progress. Additionally, start small. Tracking too many habits at once can become overwhelming and may result in losing focus.

One commonly used method for habit tracking is the classic habit tracker grid. This can be as simple as a printed sheet where you mark off each day you complete your chosen habit. Each tick mark becomes a small victory, a visual reminder of your commitment. Over time, these marks accumulate and transform into a powerful source of motivation as you glance back and see a month of filled checkboxes.

Another popular choice is utilizing journaling. By incorporating habit tracking into your daily or weekly journal entries, you add a layer of reflection to the process. This practice doesn't just track the completion of the habit but also allows you to observe patterns and note any challenges or milestones along the way. It makes the act of habit tracking a more holistic and mindful experience.

For those who are more tech-savvy, various apps and digital tools are available for habit tracking. Apps such as HabitBull and Streaks provide user-friendly interfaces and additional features like reminders, progress charts, and even community support. These apps can cater to a wide range of habits, making them versatile tools in your habit-forming arsenal. More on this will be discussed in the next section, "Utilizing Technology for Habit Formation."

When you track your habits, you also create data. This data can be incredibly revealing. For example, you may notice that you're more likely to exercise on days when you have less stressful work commitments. Or perhaps you'll see a spike in your reading habit during the weekends. This information can help you fine-tune your approach, figuring out the best times and conditions under which you thrive.

Another significant benefit of habit tracking is the enhancement of self-discipline. The mere act of tracking adds a layer of accountability. You're not just accountable to some abstract idea of who you want to be; you're accountable to the tangible evidence of your own record keeping. It creates a contract between your present self and your future self, where the daily act of tracking becomes both a promise and a proof.

Occasional lapses are inevitable, but habit tracking allows you to view these lapses in context. Being able to look back and see that you've otherwise been consistent can help mitigate the impact of a single missed day. It prevents the "all or nothing" mindset and offers a broader perspective on your journey. This way, the lapse is a small bump in the road, not a reason to abandon your path altogether.

But habit tracking isn't just about maintaining existing habits. It can also be a beneficial tool for ending bad habits. By tracking when and how often you engage in unwanted behaviors, you can start to identify patterns and triggers. This awareness is the first step in implementing effective strategies for change, as covered in Chapter 3, "Breaking Bad Habits."

Another interesting approach is pairing habit tracking with a reward system. When you hit a certain number of consecutive checkmarks or meet a specific goal, allow yourself a reward. This provides an additional layer of motivation as the satisfaction of daily success accumulates toward a bigger payoff. The reward should be something you genuinely look forward to, making the process of tracking feel less like a chore and more like an exciting game.

Engaging with others in your habit-tracking journey can amplify the benefits. Sharing your progress with friends or family, or joining a habit-tracking group, adds a level of social accountability. You benefit from the encouragement and advice of others, transforming what could be a solitary endeavor into a shared pursuit of growth. This social element can be especially powerful, as discussed in Chapter 6, "The Influence of Social Circles."

It's also essential to periodically review and adjust your habit-tracking methods. What works for you in the initial stages may need tweaking as you progress. Perhaps you'll need to add more habits to track, or maybe streamline your system if it becomes too cumbersome. Flexibility ensures that tracking remains a helpful tool rather than a rigid system that you eventually abandon.

Concisely, habit tracking is a powerful catalyst for change. It provides visibility, accountability, and motivation while offering insights into your behavior patterns. It helps you understand what works and what doesn't, making the path to developing new habits clearer and more manageable. By incorporating habit tracking into your life, you're taking a proactive step towards mastering your habits and, ultimately, your future. Keep in mind that this is a journey, and every tick mark, journal entry, or app notification brings you one step closer to the person you want to become.

Utilizing Technology for Habit Formation

Harnessing technology for habit formation can be a transformative step in your journey towards better habits. In today's digital age, our devices are more than just communication tools; they offer a plethora of applications and gadgets designed to support behavioral change. These tools can provide accountability, reminders, and analytics, empowering you to stay on track and make adjustments as needed. Yet, with so many options available, the challenge often lies in knowing how to utilize these tools effectively.

One of the most straightforward ways to integrate technology into your habit formation process is through habit-tracking apps. These applications range from simple to sophisticated, featuring various functionalities that can cater to different types of habits and user preferences. Apps like Habitica, for example, turn habit tracking into a game, where you earn rewards and level up for completing tasks. This gamification element can be incredibly motivating, particularly for those who enjoy gaming or need a fun incentive to stay committed.

Moreover, many habit-tracking apps come with built-in reminders and notifications. These features ensure that you never forget to practice a new habit or break an old one. Imagine setting a habit to drink more water; your app can ping you at regular intervals, reminding you to hydrate. Over time, these small reminders can significantly contribute to making the habit automatic.

Wearable technology such as fitness trackers and smartwatches also play a significant role. These devices can monitor various health metrics such as steps taken, calories burned, and sleep quality. Equipped with this data, you can set realistic and measurable goals. For example, if you're aiming to get fit, your fitness tracker can help you gradually increase your physical activity levels in a controlled manner, thus making the new behavior more sustainable.

Another compelling aspect of utilizing technology lies in data analysis. Many apps and devices offer analytics that visualize your progress over time. Graphs, charts, and progress reports provide valuable insights into your behaviors, allowing you to identify patterns and make informed adjustments. If you notice a dip in your performance, you can investigate the cause—whether it's a lack of motivation, external stressors, or simply a need to modify your approach.

Social features integrated into many habit-tracking technologies can also offer a community of support. Platforms often include sharing options or social networks where users can post their achievements and challenges. This adds an element of public accountability, which can be a powerful motivator. When others can see your progress, you're more likely to stick to your goals. Additionally, the encouragement and advice from like-minded individuals can provide an extra layer of support and inspiration.

Voice-activated assistants, such as Amazon's Alexa or Google Assistant, can also play a role in habit formation. You can set voice commands to remind you of your goals or use these assistants to quickly log activities in your habit-tracking app. This hands-free approach minimizes friction, making it easier to incorporate habit-related tasks into your daily routine without significant disruption.

Beyond apps and wearables, there are other technological tools worth exploring. Virtual reality (VR), for example, is being used in innovative ways to simulate scenarios for habit practice. If you struggle with public speaking, you could use VR to rehearse in front of virtual audiences, reducing anxiety and improving performance over time. These immersive experiences can accelerate habit formation by allowing you to practice in a controlled, risk-free environment.

Artificial intelligence (AI) also holds promise in this realm. AI-driven applications can tailor recommendations based on your behavior and preferences. For instance, an AI-powered app might notice that you perform better when you exercise in the morning and suggest tweaking your schedule accordingly. Personalized nudges from AI can make a significant difference in maintaining and optimizing habits.

However, it's essential to remember that technology is a tool, not a crutch. While these tools can provide invaluable support, the real work of habit formation comes from within. Consistency, effort, and a genuine desire to change are still crucial. Technology can assist and enhance your journey, but it can't walk the path for you.

Furthermore, there's the risk of becoming overly dependent on technology to the detriment of intrinsic motivation. It's beneficial to regularly evaluate whether the technology you're using is genuinely aiding your growth or if it's becoming a distraction. Sometimes, stepping back and re-evaluating your technological aids can help you stay focused on your true objectives.

Lastly, privacy is a critical consideration. When utilizing apps, wearables, and other tech solutions, ensure that your data is secure. Read privacy policies and choose tools that prioritize user confidentiality. Knowing that your data is secure allows you to focus on your habit formation journey without unnecessary concerns.

Incorporating technology into habit formation offers an exciting blend of convenience, motivation, and efficiency. When used thoughtfully, these tools can greatly enhance your ability to develop and maintain positive habits. From habit-tracking apps to wearables, voice assistants, and even AI, the possibilities are vast. The key is to find what works best for you, stay mindful of your motivations, and remain open to adaptation as you progress.

Chapter 6:
The Power of Environment

Imagine stepping into a space that nudges you toward your goals without you even noticing. That's the power of environment. Your surroundings can either propel you toward better habits or pull you back into old, destructive ones. Consider how reorganizing your physical space, like setting up a designated work area, can boost productivity and focus. But it's not just about physical spaces; your social environment plays a crucial role too. The people you regularly interact with can significantly influence your behavior patterns. Surrounding yourself with supportive, like-minded individuals can create a positive feedback loop that accelerates your habit formation. By making strategic changes to your environment, both physical and social, you effectively set the stage for success, making it easier to adopt new habits and sustain them over the long term.

Designing a Supportive Environment

When we talk about creating a life full of meaningful habits, one of the most often overlooked aspects is the environment we live in. Designing a supportive environment isn't just an afterthought—it's foundational. Our surroundings can either elevate us to new heights of productivity and well-being or keep us anchored to destructive cycles.

Consider your daily spaces: Your home, your workspace, your car, and even the digital environments you frequent. Each of these settings holds the power to shape your habits subtly yet profoundly. Let's delve into how small changes in these areas can serve as a catalyst for significant personal and professional growth.

First, let's focus on your home environment. This is the space where you spend most of your time, and it should reflect the kind of habits you want to cultivate. If you're aiming for a healthier lifestyle, seeing healthy foods at eye level in the fridge and having workout gear easily accessible can make a massive difference. Want to read more? Place books in every room instead of hiding them away on a high shelf. The goal is to make the preferred action the obvious and easy choice.

Your workspace also greatly influences your productivity and creativity. A cluttered desk can be a source of constant distraction, impeding your ability to focus. Strive for a clean, organized workspace where every item has its place. Technologies like noise-canceling headphones or apps that block distracting websites can further help in creating a conducive working atmosphere.

It's equally important to design environments that discourage bad habits. If you're trying to cut down on screen time, move your phone charger to a less convenient location. This simple change can help reduce the temptation to scroll endlessly before bed. Small modifications can yield significant results.

The social environment you navigate also plays a critical role. While you can't always control the people around you, you can control how much time you spend with those who positively or negatively influence your habits. If you're trying to adopt a new habit, consider joining a group or community with similar goals. Shared accountability can be a powerful motivator.

Think about the digital environments you frequent. We spend a significant portion of our lives in digital spaces, whether it's social media, work platforms, or entertainment services. Customize your online experiences to be more aligned with your goals. Unfollow accounts that flood your feed with distractions, install apps that remind you to take breaks, and use tools that help you stay committed to your goals.

Also, take a closer look at how you start and end your day in your environment. These are pivotal moments that set the tone for the hours to come. Design a morning routine that energizes you and an evening routine that winds you down. Minimalist spaces in the morning, free from clutter, can make the start of your day feel less stressful and more intentional. Similarly, tranquility in your evening environment can signal to your brain that it's time to relax and wind down.

While designing a supportive environment, don't overlook the power of cues and triggers. These are usually small details that might seem insignificant on their own but collectively have a massive impact. Sticky notes with motivational quotes, a screensaver with your goals, or an app to track your progress can serve as constant reminders of your larger objectives. These elements act as cues, nudging you towards productive behaviors.

However, it's crucial not to overcomplicate this process. Start with small, manageable changes and gradually build on them. The idea is not to overhaul your entire environment overnight but to continually make improvements that align with your evolving goals.

Remember, this is not just about adding things to your environment; it's also about what you should remove. If there's an item or a particular setting that habitually leads to negative behaviors, it's time to consider getting rid of it. If you find yourself binge-watching TV shows late into the night, perhaps removing the television from the bedroom might be an effective strategy.

Lastly, don't underestimate the power of aesthetics. A well-designed space that pleases your senses can have a subliminal yet powerful effect on your mood and behavior. Surround yourself with visuals, scents, and sounds that uplift your spirits. A well-lit room, some inspiring artwork, and calming scents like lavender can create an environment where your best habits are more likely to flourish.

Designing a supportive environment is a dynamic process. It's about continually assessing and tweaking your surroundings to best serve your habit-building goals. Small changes can yield substantial enhancements to your quality of life. By thoughtfully curating your physical, social, and digital environments, you're setting yourself up for lasting success in both your personal and professional life.

So, take a moment to evaluate your current surroundings and identify what's working and what isn't. Start making those incremental changes today, because a supportive environment isn't just a backdrop to your life—it's an active player in the story of your personal growth.

The Influence of Social Circles

When we talk about the power of environment in shaping our habits, we often overlook a crucial element – our social circles. The people we surround ourselves with can significantly influence our behaviors, both positive and negative. It's a concept rooted deeply in human nature. We are social creatures, inherently inclined to mimic the behaviors, attitudes, and even the emotional responses of those we consider our peers. This tendency can either be a catalyst for positive change or a barrier to breaking harmful patterns.

Imagine you aim to develop a habit of regular exercise. If your friends frequently engage in physical activities and talk about their fitness journeys with enthusiasm, you're naturally more inclined to join in. Their behavior provides a form of social proof, signaling to you that this is a worthwhile pursuit. And it's not just about peer pressure; it's also about shared experiences, encouragement, and accountability. Exercising with friends can make the habit more enjoyable and sustainable.

However, the influence of social circles isn't solely a conscious decision. There are subtler, more insidious ways people around us shape our habits. Consider smoking, for instance. If you're trying to quit but regularly spend time with friends who smoke, resisting the temptation becomes exponentially harder. Your environment isn't just about physical spaces; it's also defined by the social norms and habits of your peers.

It's important to assess your social circles critically. This isn't to say you should cut ties with people who exhibit habits you're trying to avoid. Rather, awareness is the first step. Understand how these individuals influence your behavior. Recognize situations where you might be more susceptible to falling back into old patterns due to their presence.

Strategies for Leveraging Social Influence

How can you turn this ubiquitous social influence to your advantage? One effective strategy is to seek out accountability partners. Find someone who shares your goals and is equally committed to achieving them. Whether it's a colleague aiming to improve productivity or a friend striving for a healthier lifestyle, mutual accountability can reinforce commitment.

If you don't have immediate friends or family who align with your goals, consider joining a community group. Online forums, local clubs, and social media groups can provide a supportive network of like-minded individuals. These communities can offer insights, share their own challenges and victories, and provide a robust support system.

Another approach is to cultivate an environment of open dialogue with your current social circles. Express your goals and the reasons behind them. Sometimes, merely articulating your intentions can create a positive ripple effect. When your friends understand why you're making certain changes, they're more likely to support you and, potentially, even join you.

The influence of social circles extends to professional settings as well. In a workplace, the habits of co-workers can affect productivity, adherence to schedules, and even stress levels. Surrounding yourself with colleagues who maintain a strong work ethic and positive attitude can bolster your own professional habits. Proactively seeking mentors within your organization can provide guidance and exemplify desirable behaviors.

Stringent boundaries can sometimes be necessary, especially if your social circle involves individuals whose habits are in direct conflict with your goals. For example, if you're aiming to lose weight, consistently dining out with friends who indulge in unhealthy eating can be counterproductive. This doesn't mean severing relationships but rather setting limits. Perhaps suggest alternative activities that align better with your goals, such as hiking or cooking healthy meals together.

The Ripple Effect of Positive Habits

It's also worth noting that influencing your social circles works both ways. By adopting positive habits, you can inspire those around you to do the same. This means your personal growth isn't just a solitary effort; it can have a broader impact, creating a ripple effect. When you lead a healthier, more productive life, your friends and family might start to notice and feel motivated to make changes themselves.

This phenomenon is evident in various aspects of life. For example, when someone commits to personal development and starts reaping its benefits, it's natural for others to take note. They may seek advice, join the journey, or simply try to emulate the positive behaviors they observe. Whether it's reading more, adopting a regular exercise routine, or practicing gratitude, your habits can serve as a powerful example for your social circle.

Navigating Social Pressures and Expectations

Not all social influences are beneficial. Social pressures and expectations can sometimes be detrimental to habit formation. It's crucial to recognize these influences and develop strategies to mitigate their impact. For instance, if your friends regularly pressure you to stay out late, potentially disrupting your sleep and productivity routines, decision-making becomes pivotal. Learn to assert your boundaries and prioritize your goals, even if it means occasionally standing apart from the group.

Dealing with social pressures often requires a blend of tact and firmness. You don't have to alienate yourself or come across as judgmental. Instead, communicate your reasons clearly and respectfully. Over time, true friends will likely understand and respect your choices, and you might even find that some follow suit.

Furthermore, it can be helpful to shift focus towards the long-term benefits of your goals. Social scenarios are often immediate and tempting, but keeping your eye on the bigger picture helps reinforce your commitment. Recall why you started, and let that conviction guide your choices, even in the face of social pressures.

Your social circles play an undeniably vital role in shaping your environment and, subsequently, your habits. By mindfully selecting and cultivating relationships that align with your goals, leveraging accountability, and navigating pressures with grace, you can harness this influence to create a supportive, motivating ambiance conducive to personal and professional growth. The power of social circles in habit formation underscores the broader theme of environmental influence, reminding us that the people we choose to surround ourselves with can either bolster or hinder our efforts towards a better life.

Chapter 7:
Long-Term Maintenance

Embarking on the journey of habit transformation is only the beginning; the real challenge lies in sustaining those changes over the long haul. Long-term maintenance is anchored in vigilance and commitment, acting as the bridge between initial enthusiasm and enduring success. To avoid relapse, it's crucial to anticipate potential pitfalls and develop strategies to address them proactively. Celebrating progress, no matter how small, fuels your motivation and reminds you of how far you've come. Remember, each day is an opportunity to reaffirm your commitment, and it's by regularly reassessing and adjusting your habits that they truly become a part of who you are. Continuity, combined with a little self-compassion, paves the way for lasting change and a transformed life.

Avoiding Relapse

Long-term maintenance of good habits requires vigilance, especially when trying to avoid relapse. Relapse can be incredibly disheartening, but it's essential to remember that it's a common part of the journey towards lasting change. To truly understand how to avoid falling back into old habits, we need to delve into several strategies and mindsets that enable resilience and sustained progress.

One of the first things to recognize is that a relapse does not signify failure; it's an opportunity for growth and learning. When faced with a setback, take a moment to reflect. What triggered the relapse? Recognizing the specific circumstances that led you astray helps build awareness, which is the first step to preventing future lapses.

Moreover, it's crucial to adjust your mindset. Instead of focusing on perfection, emphasize progress. Understand that long-term change is a journey, not a destination. Small, consistent steps compound over time, creating significant shifts in behavior and mindset. This perspective helps cultivate patience and reduces the all-or-nothing mentality that often precipitates relapse.

Accountability can be a powerful tool in avoiding relapse. Whether it's a close friend, family member, or a support group, sharing your goals and progress with others enhances commitment. Social accountability creates a web of support that can catch you before you fall, providing both encouragement and constructive feedback.

Maintaining an environment that supports your new habits is equally important. We've already discussed the power of environment earlier in this book, but it's worth reiterating here. A supportive environment reduces friction and makes it easier to stick to your new routines. Ensure that your surroundings are conducive to your goals, whether that means removing temptations or creating physical reminders of your commitment.

Another valuable strategy is to continuously review and reinforce your "why." Understanding the deeper reasons behind your desire for change can reignite motivation and keep you on track. When faced with the temptation to revert to old habits, revisit your core values and goals. This anchor can provide the strength needed to stay committed, even in challenging times.

Equally important is self-compassion. Be kind to yourself during this process. Self-blame and negativity only compound stress and make relapse more likely. Instead, treat yourself with the same compassion you would offer a friend. Acknowledge the challenge, forgive yourself for any missteps, and recommit to your goals.

Additionally, setting up frequent "check-ins" with yourself can help in early identification of potential relapses. These check-ins can be as simple as daily journaling or a more structured weekly review. Assess what's working, what's not, and make necessary adjustments. This habit of regular self-reflection ensures that you stay aligned with your objectives and can course-correct when needed.

Learning coping mechanisms for stress and anxiety is also pivotal. Often, relapse occurs during periods of high stress. Developing skills like mindfulness, meditation, and deep-breathing exercises can help manage stress and reduce the urge to return to old habits for comfort. Incorporating these practices into your daily routine can build emotional resilience.

Physical health plays a vital role in avoiding relapse. Ensure you're getting adequate sleep, eating nutritious foods, and engaging in regular physical activity. Physical well-being directly influences mental health, making it easier to maintain discipline and focus. A healthy body supports a healthy mind, creating a positive feedback loop that bolsters your resolve.

Specific goal setting can further fortify your efforts. SMART goals (Specific, Measurable, Achievable, Relevant, Time-bound) provide clarity and structure, making your objectives more tangible and attainable. Break down larger goals into smaller, manageable milestones. This approach not only makes progress visible but also creates a sense of accomplishment, which fuels ongoing motivation.

The act of celebrating small victories shouldn't be underestimated either. Recognizing and rewarding your progress, no matter how minor, reinforces positive behavior. Each milestone celebrated builds confidence and reminds you of how far you've come, making you more resilient against future relapses.

Lastly, develop contingency plans for unavoidable high-risk situations. Life is unpredictable, and there will be times when you are tested. Having a plan in place for these moments can make a significant difference. Whether it's a strategy for dealing with social pressures or a distraction technique for cravings, being prepared equips you to handle potential threats to your progress.

In summary, avoiding relapse in the long term requires a multifaceted approach. By cultivating a growth mindset, leveraging accountability, maintaining a supportive environment, and practicing self-compassion, you create a robust defense against old habits. Regular self-check-ins, stress management techniques, physical health, specific goal setting, celebrating small victories, and having contingency plans all contribute to sustaining your new habits and avoiding relapse.

Ultimately, remember that relapses are part of the process. They offer a valuable learning experience and an opportunity to recommit to your goals with renewed vigor. With these strategies in place, you are well-equipped to navigate the journey of long-term maintenance and continue moving forward toward a more empowered, habit-driven life.

Celebrating Progress

When embarking on the journey of long-term maintenance, it's crucial to remember that the road to sustaining new habits isn't a straight line, but a winding path filled with twists and turns. Amidst these challenges, one of the most powerful tools at your disposal is the act of celebrating progress. It's not just about patting yourself on the back; celebrating progress serves as a motivational fuel that keeps the engine of habit change running smoothly.

Think of celebrating progress as anchoring a ship. It grounds you in your journey, preventing the winds of doubt and the storms of relapse from steering you off course. Each milestone achieved, no matter how small, is a testament to your commitment and perseverance. But how exactly should one go about celebrating progress?

First and foremost, recognize that progress isn't always linear. There will be days when you take two steps forward and one step back, and that's perfectly okay. It's important to acknowledge and celebrate even the smallest wins. Did you manage to get out of bed early three days in a row? That's progress. Did you resist the temptation to skip the gym once this week? Another win.

Understanding that progress can take many forms helps cultivate a mindset of appreciation and positivity. This shift in perspective is invaluable because it reinforces the belief that you are capable of change. It builds a positive feedback loop that can make sustaining new habits much easier over the long haul.

Moreover, the way you celebrate your progress matters. This can be as simple or as elaborate as you want it to be. The key is to choose celebrations that are meaningful to you. Some people may find joy in journaling their wins, while others may prefer treating themselves to a small gift or a favorite activity. The celebration itself isn't as important as the act of acknowledging your effort and triumph.

For some, public recognition can add an extra layer of accountability and satisfaction. Sharing your progress with friends, family, or even social media communities that support your goals can provide additional motivation. When others recognize your achievements, it can validate your efforts and spur you on to continue pushing forward.

However, don't fall into the trap of comparison. Your journey is unique to you, and so is your progress. Celebrate your milestones on your terms and avoid comparing your pace or accomplishments with others. Everyone's path is different, and what matters most is that you are moving forward in your own way and at your own speed.

A powerful method to celebrate progress is by creating visual reminders of your achievements. This could be a simple chart, a vision board, or even a collection of photos capturing moments of success. Visual cues serve as constant reminders of how far you've come and can reignite your motivation during challenging times.

Another effective approach is to reflect on your progress regularly. Set aside time each week or month to review your achievements and lessons learned. This reflection helps solidify your progress and provides an opportunity to adjust your strategies if needed. Celebrate these moments of introspection as they reinforce your commitment to long-term maintenance.

While celebrating progress, it's essential to maintain a balance. Don't let celebrations become a distraction or a reason to become complacent. The goal is to celebrate in a way that fuels further progress rather than hindering it. This balance ensures that celebrations are a source of motivation and not a detour from your objectives.

Parents and educators have long known the importance of positive reinforcement in promoting desired behaviors. Similarly, self-reinforcement—through celebrating your wins—encourages the continued practice of new habits. This approach is backed by psychological principles that emphasize the role of rewards in habit formation and maintenance.

Incorporate celebrations into your long-term strategy by setting specific milestones to reach. These milestones can be periods of consistent behavior, achieving a particular goal, or even surviving a particularly challenging scenario while sticking to your new habits. By setting these benchmarks, you create a structured yet flexible framework for recognizing and celebrating progress.

Consider the concept of "look how far you've come" moments. These are opportunities to pause and reflect on your journey from where you started to where you are now. These reflections often reveal progress that wasn't immediately apparent and provide a deeper sense of accomplishment and motivation to continue.

Finally, remember that celebrating progress is about more than just individual milestones. It's also about recognizing the broader impact of your sustained habits. Have your new habits improved your relationships, increased your productivity, or enhanced your overall well-being? Celebrate these broader achievements as they highlight the far-reaching effects of your efforts.

In summary, celebrating progress is a fundamental aspect of long-term maintenance. It reinforces your commitment, boosts your motivation, and provides a positive feedback loop that makes sustaining new habits more manageable. Embrace each win, no matter how small, and use these celebrations as stepping stones on your path to lasting change. Your journey is ongoing, and every step forward is worth celebrating.

Conclusion

Throughout the journey of this book, we've delved into the intricate science of habits, the psychology behind making lasting changes, and the actionable strategies to both break bad habits and build good ones. It's now time to tie everything together and focus on the path ahead. Change isn't easy, but armed with the knowledge and tools you've gained, you're more than capable of transforming your life.

The first step in any journey is awareness, and by understanding the formation of habits, you've begun to take control. Knowledge alone isn't enough, though. You need to apply it consistently. This isn't about overnight revolutions; it's about steady, deliberate evolution. Make small changes, observe their impacts, and adjust as necessary.

Motivation is crucial, but it's not a constant. Some days you'll feel incredibly driven; other days, less so. That's natural, and it's okay. What matters is not how you feel on any given day but the actions you continue to take. Use the strategies discussed – such as developing a supportive environment and leveraging technology – to maintain momentum even when your intrinsic motivation wanes.

Breaking bad habits can often feel like an uphill battle. We all have patterns and triggers embedded deep within our lives that make change difficult. Yet, difficult doesn't mean impossible. With careful identification of these triggers and consistent interruption of the patterns, you can dismantle even the most stubborn habits. Remember, change often requires patience and persistence. Don't be too hard on yourself if progress seems slow – it's part of the process.

On the flip side, *building good habits* is equally challenging, yet tremendously rewarding. Crafting routines and creating new habit loops can transform the mundane into the extraordinary. Each small victory builds a foundation for the next, creating a ripple effect throughout your life. As discussed, ensuring your environment supports these changes is paramount. Your surroundings, both physical and social, play a pivotal role in your success.'

One of the most powerful tools at your disposal is **habit tracking**. Monitoring your progress not only provides valuable insights but also serves as a powerful motivator. Whether it's through a journal, an app, or a simple checklist, consistently tracking your habits allows you to see incremental improvements that might otherwise go unnoticed. These small wins build confidence and reinforce your commitment to change.

Celebrating progress is often overlooked but vitally important. Take the time to acknowledge your achievements, no matter how small. This acknowledgment reinforces your efforts and provides a boost to your motivation. Remember, the journey to change isn't solely about reaching a destination but also about appreciating the progress along the way.

Change is a dynamic process. The strategies and techniques that work today may need to be adjusted tomorrow. Stay flexible and open to experimentation. This adaptability will serve you well as you encounter new challenges and opportunities on your path to a better life.

Long-term maintenance is about more than avoiding relapse. It's about sustaining momentum and continuously evolving. As you build and refine your habits, you'll find new areas for growth and improvement. This ongoing commitment to personal development ensures that your journey doesn't end but evolves.

One last piece of advice: be kind to yourself. Change is hard, and setbacks are part of the process. Rather than viewing them as failures, see them as opportunities to learn and grow. Each setback provides valuable insights that can inform and improve your ongoing efforts.

In conclusion, forming better habits is a powerful tool for transforming both your personal and professional life. Through understanding, strategic planning, and consistent application, you have the power to create lasting change. The journey may be challenging, but the rewards are immense. You're not just changing habits; you're reshaping your future. Take these insights, apply them with courage, and embrace the transformative impact of effective habit formation. Your best life awaits.

Appendix A:
Appendix

This appendix is intended to provide additional resources, tools, and insights that complement the chapters on habit formation, change psychology, and sustainable growth. Included in this appendix is guidance and support as you embark. on your journey to better habits and a more fulfilling life.

Resource List

Here are some resources that can provide further information and support:

- *Books:* There are several influential books on habit formation and personal growth that can offer deeper insights. Notable authors in this field have written extensively on the subjects covered in this book.

- *Websites:* Many websites offer tools and articles on developing positive habits and breaking negative ones. They can serve as supplementary material to expand your knowledge.

- *Apps:* Technology can be a powerful ally in habit formation. There are a variety of apps designed to help you track your progress, set reminders, and stay motivated.

Templates and Worksheets

Included are several template and worksheet ideas that can be created in Excel or Word to assist you in planning and monitoring your habit changes:

1. *Habit Tracking Sheet:* Use this to keep a daily log of your habits, both new and existing, to visualize your progress.

2. *Goal Setting Worksheet:* Outline your long-term and short-term goals, breaking them down into manageable actions.

3. *Environmental Checklist:* A guide to help you modify your environment in ways that support your new habits.

Frequently Asked Questions (FAQs)

Compiled are responses to some common questions that people often have when trying to change their habits:

- *How long does it take to form a new habit?* Research suggests it can take anywhere from 18 days to over two months to solidify a new habit, depending on complexity and individual factors.

- *What if I relapse?* Setbacks are part of the process. Recognize what triggered the relapse and adjust your strategies accordingly.

- *How do I deal with lack of motivation?* Identifying your underlying motivations and keeping reminders of your goals can be incredibly helpful.

Additional Reading

Sometimes a single book isn't enough. Here are recommendations for further reading that can enhance your understanding of habit formation and maintenance:

- *Deep Work:* Focused on overcoming distractions and building highly productive habits.

- *The Willpower Instinct:* A deep dive into the science of self-control and how to strengthen it.

- *Atomic Habits:* Insightful strategies for making small, incremental changes that lead to big results over time.

Support Networks

Remember that you don't have to go through this journey alone. Engaging with supportive communities can offer encouragement and accountability:

- *Online Forums:* There are various forums and social media groups dedicated to personal development and habit formation.

- *Local Meetups:* Look for local groups that meet to discuss goals, progress, and provide mutual support.

- *Mental Health Professionals:* Sometimes professional guidance can offer new perspectives and tailored strategies.

Hopefully this appendix serves as a valuable resource as you apply the principles discussed in this book. Remember, the path to lasting change is a journey, not a destination. Leverage these tools, remain resilient, and keep your vision for a better life at the forefront of everything you do.